Letters to God—From Teenagers

Letters to God
from teenagers

Edited by Kevin Jones-Prendergast

Scripture texts used in this work are taken from the NEW AMERICAN BIBLE, copyright © 1970, by the Confraternity of Christian Doctrine, Washington, D.C., are used by permission of copyright owner. All rights reserved.

Cover, illustrations and book design by Julie Van Leeuwen.

Photographs by Cliff Koehler.

Photographs on pages 56 and 90 by Julie Van Leeuwen.

Back cover photo by Eugene Carmichael, S.J.

SBN 0-912228-56-3

For Tom Shea and Jerry Grosh,
who helped me in the journey
from adolescence to adulthood.

. . . carmina non prius audita
Musarum sacerdos virginibus puerisque
canto.

. . . I, priest of the Muses, sing songs
never heard before to young men and
women.

Horace, *Odes*, III. 1

Acknowledgements

I wish to express here my deep gratitude to the many people who have made this book possible:

Jim Willig, whose infectious trust and enthusiasm encouraged us to experiment with letters to God for the very first time;

Jane Myers, who believed that these letters should be made available to a larger audience and who actively supported me in this project;

Tracey Robson Sandman, who contributed much to the thematic categories at an early stage;

Tom James, who helped shape many of the ideas expressed in the Introduction;

Bill Creed, S.J., Jerry Grosh, S.J., and Michael Sparough, S.J., each of whom reviewed the manuscript at various stages and offered important suggestions;

Tom Diehl, S.J., who, by encouraging creativity in the youth retreat program at the Jesuit Renewal Center made possible an atmosphere of discovery;

my wife, Maggie, who not only patiently endured the chaos created by this book, but who also made ongoing suggestions about its content;

and, finally, the thousands of students who have enriched my life immeasurably over the past five years and who have left behind the legacy of these poems, prayers, psalms.

I also wish to thank Karen Hurley and Jeremy Harrington, O.F.M., of St. Anthony Messenger Press, who have made the completion of this work more of a delight than I anticipated.

Contents

Introduction

I feel privileged to share with you this collection of "letters to God" written by high school students while on retreat at the Jesuit Renewal Center, Milford, Ohio. When we began three years ago asking young people to write these letters, none of us foresaw the result of our "experiment." Frankly, I was skeptical of the whole idea; it struck me as too juvenile an exercise for sophisticated teenagers. Wasn't a letter to God something you would ask a first-grader to do?

The first retreatants we asked to write such letters was a group of 40 football players from a local high school. During the first afternoon of the retreat, we had discussed faith, God and the Church in small groups. What we heard was a good deal of antipathy toward organized religion. My expectations were therefore quite low that evening when we gave directions on writing a letter to God.

I was completely unprepared for what happened a little later when some of the students read their letters aloud as part of our liturgy together. I heard moving expressions of trust in God, outpourings of thanks and praise, profound desires for meaning and closeness to the Lord. A much deeper level of personal experience and feeling emerged through these letters than had been revealed through discussions among peers earlier in the day. This experience forced me to rethink some of my fundamental assumptions about adolescents and about the ways in which God can work.

All of the letters in this collection were written within the context of one-day or over-night youth retreats. The authors range in age from 15 to 20.

The format developed as part of our original experiment with the letters was very simple and has not been significantly altered since: After a brief witness talk by one or two of the retreat staff in which they share their personal faith experience, we describe the prayer exercise we have in mind:

We now invite you to spend a few minutes writing a letter to God. This may sound corny at first, but we ask you to try it. Just write down whatever is on your mind or in your heart. Maybe you would like to tell God how you feel about him. Maybe you would like to thank him, or argue with him, or ask him for something. You may just want to talk over your life with him, as you would with a friend. You might even want to tell him you don't believe in him, if that's how you feel. Just relax and do what feels right to you. We'll put on some soft music; when you're finished, feel free to leave the room. Take as much time as you'd like.

Occasionally, we have also asked the retreatants to write a letter *from* God, imagining how God would respond to their prayers. Sometimes both letters were written at one sitting; at other times the letter *to* God was written on the first day and the letter *from* God at the close of the retreat. A sample of these pairs of letters is presented in the final section.

Because we were interested in using some of the letters as part of a liturgy planned for later in the day, we began to add a further direction at the end of the explanation above. We made clear that no one should feel compelled or coerced to make his or her letter public, but indicated that this option of sharing was available. A fair number of students are always willing to allow their letters to be read publicly at the liturgy.

This has proven to be a powerful experience for all retreatants. It must be similar to the reaction in the early Church when an epistle arrived and was read for the first time. The letters have served to complement whatever Scripture readings are used and they help make the Word more immediate and personal.

We have also asked that all letters turned in for reading be anonymous. This fact no doubt makes it easier to share such personal feelings with peers.

As time went on, we also began extending an open-ended invitation to our retreatants to allow their letters to be shared with a wider audience. Initially we intended to use the letters at workshops for youth ministers, meetings for parents and so forth. Many retreatants did choose to leave their letters with us to use as we saw fit. Over the years, we have thus collected more than 5,000 letters; it is from this vast number that the present collection of about 100 is drawn. The generosity of our young friends has made such a collection possible.

In editing these letters for publication, I have taken every pain to insure anonymity for their authors. All biographical data have been altered, names have been omitted, and specific facts have been changed. I do not believe these alterations have in any way affected the sense of a letter or its thematic content. I do feel I owe this much, however, to our friends who have entrusted to us a part of themselves.

Preparing these letters for publication presented many challenges. The first was simply to catalogue each of the more than 5,000 letters at my disposal. Many more categories and subcategories could be imagined, but for the purposes of this volume six basic thematic divisions have been chosen: (1) the search for purpose; (2) doubt and suffering; (3) relationships: love and loneliness; (4) petitions; (5) thanks and new awareness; (6) dialogues with God.

And then came the difficulty of choosing one letter over another. I believe that the 100 letters I have selected represent a fair cross-section of the total collection.

A special problem was presented by the condition of the letters themselves. Written on half-sheets of notebook paper in pencil, usually within the space of 10 or 15 minutes, the letters are an English teacher's nightmare. Infinitives regularly find themselves split, past tenses go astray, syntax resembles glossolalia, and spelling becomes an exercise in creative expression.

My editorial decision has been to regularize the spelling and to supply missing words where the sense demands. Where syntax has been hopelessly garbled, an attempt has been made to restore meaning. The letters are, however, substantially as they were first written. I have changed only those items which seemed likely to distract from the real message of an author. Purists may be offended; but then again few purists last long in youth ministry.

How to Use These Letters

These letters to God lend themselves to a variety of uses:

The letters can be used by an individual *for personal reflection and prayer.* The letters can be approached as one would approach the Psalms, as articulations of the different states and feelings one experiences in the course of a relationship with the Lord.

We have used the letters extensively *in liturgical settings and for prayer services* of many kinds. They can be read as communion thanksgiving meditations; as part of a reconciliation service; or as a means for leading a small group into prayer together.

In the classroom or the religious education program, the letters can be a starting point for discussion and sharing. They can certainly complement other materials being used in the study of sacraments, Scripture, Christology, ecclesiology and so on. Because of their ability to evoke deep resonances in adolescents, these letters can speak to areas of the person which purely academic materials might not touch.

The letters can also serve an interpersonal function *in dialogue between parents and teenagers.* Suggestions for using the letters as a means to such dialogue are included at the end of each section. Sharing reactions to the letters and talking openly about the questions of belief which occur in the letters can prove valuable tools for improving communications within a family.

Finally, religious educators may find the letters a valuable window into the world of the adolescent. They contain a great many clues as to "where young people are" today. They are rich ground *for theological reflections and for gaining insight into the nature of faith development.*

Some Theological Reflections

These letters demonstrate irrefutably to me that adolescents are constantly questioning, seeking and probing; that they are not uninterested in the ultimate issues raised by the Christian gospel. And, as I mentioned above, the letters to God have significantly influenced my development as a youth minister over the past several years. I have been forced, because of them, to develop some new understandings of my role as minister, of what the Church means, of what adolescents need from the Church in the course of their faith development.

When we accept adolescents where they are and as they are, we make it possible that, *later on,* they will develop a desire for sound theology, for content, for teaching. This is not, however, the first step in the process.

Therefore, it is my belief that any program of religious education which relies strictly upon a *content model* is doomed from the start to failure. Too often, the cart is put before the horse: We teach advanced sacramental theology to sophomores who do not believe in sacraments or have a genuine experience of Church; we spend months on Scripture and biblical criticism with students who aren't sure they believe in God; we teach Christian morality to teens who do not believe that Jesus ever lived. We ignore the live questions and experiences which students have in favor of a curriculum which insists that adolescents first possess a certain quantity of knowledge.

In contrast to this content model, we need a highly *incarnational* approach. As these letters reveal, every adolescent has real life-experiences whose faith dimensions are only waiting to be articulated: experiences of loneliness, love, suffering, joy, wonder, decision-making. What is necessary, I believe, is a model of ministry and religious education which holds these human experiences in reverence as the focal point of God's Word of revelation.

Likewise, we must not treat lightly the criticisms which adolescents make of the Church. Much of their cynicism could, of course, be written off as the "typical" adolescent dislike for institutions and preference for ideal, utopian dreams. Such a cavalier attitude, however, overlooks some of the real shortcomings of the Church which ought to evoke a desire for change.

Foremost among these shortcomings is the *lack of community* in most of our congregations. Adolescents, indeed all persons, desire a place where they can feel accepted, affirmed, cherished; a group of people who support one another actively in a common vision; an environment for the celebration of all truly holy moments in one's life. In places where these elements exist within a local church, adolescents demonstrate a genuine excitement about worshiping with the body of believers.

Connected with this desire for community is the need for *credible adult faith models*. Adolescents are intensely curious about how adults came to their major decisions in life: vocation, beliefs, values, faith relationship. They desire, in my experience, to hear adults talk about why they believe in God and how they relate to God in their everyday life. When adolescents are met with sermons or generalities instead of honest and direct sharing, it is little wonder that they grow cold toward the Church (meaning *us*, since we are the Church).

Finally, in attempting to assess where adolescents are with regard to the Lord, I think it is unwise to apply the same criteria to the faith of a junior in high school as one would to the belief of an adult Christian. After reflecting on the thousands of letters to God we have collected, I am convinced that most adolescents cannot be described as believing Christians; they can more accurately be characterized as deists who may be moving in the direction of explicit Christianity.

Only a handful of the adolescents I have met relate strongly to the person of Jesus or seem to have a personal relationship with him; I believe very few teens would offer as a rationale for their moral behavior that they are following the path of Jesus or that they have discerned his Spirit at work. The trinitarian experience of God is simply, for the most part, absent. God is seen much more as a benevolent force or cosmic source of meaning and purpose than as Lord or personal savior.

To say this is not to pass judgment on the adolescent image of God; rather it is to encourage an awareness of the changing nature of adolescent faith. I have met few authentic teenage atheists. What appears as unbelief or heresy to some may, in an adolescent, be a necessary step on the journey toward an adult relationship with the God we profess as Christians.

In this connection, a useful analogy may be made between the letters to God and the Psalms. It is possible to read the Psalms as the articulation of various moments in one person's relationship with God. Surely few would accuse the psalmist of heresy because he at times curses God or questions the very fact of God's love for his people. Likewise, in reading these letters to God, one can imagine that a single person could give voice to every nuance of feeling found in this volume—both the most intense joy and the most poignant sorrow, both radical alienation and great intimacy.

Also like the Psalms, the great majority of these letters return, even after expressions of acute doubt or pain, to a fundamental acknowledgement of God's presence and care. No matter how lonely the journey at this moment, a note of hope emerges even in many of the darkest letters: the hope that God will indeed be found at the end.

A Note to Teens

At home, in school, at church, everyone tells you who God is. You've heard a lot about him all your life. But who do *you* think God is? What does he mean in your life right now?

As you read through these letters to God, maybe you'll find some echoes of the way you feel. Perhaps you'll find yourself thinking that you would have said exactly the same thing as one of the teenage authors of these letters. I invite you to try out the different voices and feelings and beliefs that are contained in this book. And ask yourself, "Which ones really fit the person I am?"

Let these letters be a mirror of your real self. Allow them to become your prayers — prayers you can pray when you feel happy or down or when you're thinking about where your life is going.

I invite you, also, to think about sharing your reactions to these letters with your parents. That might sound strange, but it could be the beginning of something new in your relationship with them. You might discover some things about them that you never guessed were there. I invite you to give it a try.

A Note to Parents

In my work directing retreats for adolescents, I have talked with many parents who express concern over their teenagers' apparent lack of faith. Parents are anxious or hurt when their sons and daughters stop going to church or when they give voice to cynicism about organized religion. Parents can easily begin to think that they have somehow failed in their responsibilities.

What I have learned from students on retreat, and particularly from the thousands of letters to God they have written, is that external appearances are quite deceptive. It is crucial to distinguish a person's attitude toward the Church from that same person's underlying relationship with God. Frequently, with adolescents, organized religion is (at least temporarily) rejected, while the search for God goes on actively deep within a person's heart.

Furthermore, the natural and desirable development of adolescents includes the growth of an incisive critical faculty. The old beliefs of childhood must be reexamined or cast away before an adult faith can be fully appropriated. Many teens seem to make this transition with relative ease, experiencing no great trauma in the process. Others, however, must undergo great travail and inner turmoil (and subject their parents to the same) before they reach adult decisions about their faith.

What is required in response, I believe, is not sermonizing or lecturing, but rather listening and empathy. What would it be like if more parents shared with their teenagers their own beliefs, and the struggles, doubts and hopes that mark their relationship with the Lord?

I encourage you as a parent to make use of the suggestions for dialogue presented in the text. Such dialogue cannot, of course, be forced, but it might lead to a richer understanding and acceptance between yourself and your teens. Above all, I encourage you to share yourself—for that is the gift adolescents most desire.

As the hind longs
   for the running waters,
so my soul longs
   for you, O God.
Athirst is my soul for God,
   the living God.
When shall I go and behold
   the face of God?

Psalm 42:2-3

I. The Search for Purpose

Too much has certainly been made of adolescence as the "turbulent years," as the period of groping, self-doubt, confusion. One must admit, however, that these years are at least a time of transition. Rites of passage do occur, and not merely in the biological or sexual realm. The passage must also be made from the faith of childhood to an adult belief.

Adolescents are at an uncomfortable juncture. They have rejected (or at least challenged) the faith and the Church of their early years, but they have not yet fully appropriated their own beliefs, mores, or relationship with God. It is a time for trying on various attitudes about the ultimate questions of life. Teenagers find themselves searching, questioning, wondering why they exist, pondering what the meaning of their life-journey will be.

The letters in this section strike me as profoundly existential. God is seen here as, above all else, a question mark, as an unknown, as someone dimly perceived but as yet undiscovered. The authors are on a quest, and their search is for coherence, meaning, purpose.

I heard a woodpecker this morning

Hey,

Hello. I heard a woodpecker this morning. I wandered out into the woods during a break and came into an open area. I heard the birds singing and the woodpecker. But you know that. It feels good to be able to say it to you.

Come to me.

I believe that, if I can know you, I can follow you through anything.

You know my thirst for purpose, for meaning.

Tell me your will, love me, give me significance.

Seventeen years

Dear God,

Seventeen years have flown by quickly. Ten times 17 years from now, I will be long dead. After five times 17 years I will probably be dead. The time certainly flies by quickly.

When I'm dead, someone like me will be wondering how fast the time will fly.

I hope that I will be a productive member of society while I exist.

This isn't a time for indecision for me as much as apprehension.

I am apprehensive about whether I'll be a valuable link in the massive chain of society, held together by productive people; or will I simply be one of the holes in between?

In another batch of 17 years, I will know.

Please add meaning to my life

Dear God,

Please add meaning to my life. I'm so confused. I reach out to find a purpose and reason for existing, yet I become totally confused. Whether I am mind or soul or body only, I know I exist—but why? Why and how am I here? Every time I try to figure it out, I get lost and confused. There must be someone or something beyond, I guess. But how did you come into existence? Damn, it's confusing. How can I know you if I don't know myself? Yet how can I know myself if I don't know my creator? Life and existence is one big question for me. Somewhere lies the answer. I really want to search for the answer. It just confuses me and hurts my mind, though. God, wherever or whoever you may be, please help me. Even though you don't want to give me the answer yet, someday please let me know what life is all about. Give me hope, and please pick me up when I fall in my quest for the truth.

Thanks. . .

At a crossroad

Dear God,

    I'm asking you once again for your help. Here I stand, at a crossroad in my life, unsure of which road I should take. Whichever I take, though, I know you will be with me, guiding me, giving me strength.

    I've made it this far; I know I can make it the rest of the way, but not without your help. Please, stay with me: Comfort me when I'm sad. Celebrate with me when I'm happy. Give me strength when I'm weak. Congratulate me when I'm successful.

    Me and you, Lord—all the way.

Sometimes I feel
so lonely

Dear God,

   I need you. I need your help,
guidance, and most of all your love.
Sometimes I feel so lonely. I'm always
worried that I'm doing the wrong things
in my life. So many times I am so
confused, I feel like just dying. I love my
friends and I hate to hurt anyone. Please
help me to be strong and develop into a
good Christian.
   Most of all, though, God, I want to
thank you for all that you have given me.
I really am very lucky to have the things I
do. It's just hard sometimes to look at
the bright side. I always have so many
things on my mind. I can't think straight.
Please stay by me. I love you. Help me to
express my love to others.
   Thank you.

Commitment
is a very scary thing

Hi God,

   Although I haven't communicated
with you in a while, I thought that it was
about time I let you know my feelings
toward you. I am not sorry that I haven't
become fully aware of you yet, because I
am still searching for your importance in
my life. Someone put it this way: To
question one's faith is to care. So I just
want you to know that apathy hasn't set
in; it's just that I'm not ready yet. To me
the word commitment is a very scary
thing. If I commit myself to something, I
want to do a good job—my heart and
soul have to be involved. So don't panic.
You aren't losing a sheep; you are
gaining a ponderer of the faith. I just
need time to think, so hang in there and
I'll get back to you.

                    Thinking of you . . .

You seem to be testing me

Dear God,

Why me? What have I ever done to deserve this? I've been good, I haven't done anything terribly wrong. I don't understand! All I want is a reason why. I want to know you better, I want to be closer, but you seem to be testing me, seeing how far I can be pushed, how much I can stand. Please help me, I need something to lean on. Help me!

Signed,

Confused

I am tired of waste

God,

Hi. I would like to get to know you. You are like a lost friend to me. I want to find you. I want to share with you. I want to share you with other people. Please help me to find you, God. I am tired of waste; I am tired of the bad. I need to be alive and honest. Help me to live up to myself. Guide me, God, toward your goodness.

I need to be open and unhindered with humanity. I can't stand the creeping loneliness anymore. I want to be as I was meant to be. I want to fulfill myself. I want the love and happiness you bring. I know I will find you someday, but I need to stop waiting. I can't live alone anymore. I need to feel, to express emotion, to love without fear. I know you will come to me, God. I want to try to make it soon. I'll be seeing you, Lord. Let me understand.

Thank you . . .

All I want is a chance

God,

I am confused as hell. All I want is to be me. Fully and completely. Why do people judge me before I begin? All I want is a chance.

I am a young teenager

Dear God?

I am a young teenager. I don't get along with my parents. I argue with them, but I don't really like this. Sure I've done dumb things in the past—I robbed that gas station and we got caught. But I never said I was sorry until now. I have trouble with school and work, too, but I know I can get through if you help me.

Sincerely yours . . .

I can't find my gift, God

Dear God,

I would like to tell you that, even though I do a lot wrong and sometimes talk as if you're not real important to me, you are. When I'm alone, I think about you. I am really amazed how you made everything. The things you created are so beautiful and so complex—all things have a purpose.

That's one of my problems. What's my purpose in living? Parents say that every person has one special gift God gives them and that their purpose is to use that gift fully. I can't find my gift, God, and I'd appreciate it if you could help me. It's so hard to find the true me.

Please know, God, that I try to be a good Christian and to follow your ways, but it's a hard road to take.

Thank you, Lord, for the gift of my friends. For my family, too, I am always grateful, especially for my parents' love and understanding. Thanks for being there and for being you.

We are more than pawns

Dear Lord,

I know that we are more than pawns in your own little game of chess. I believe that there is meaning in life and that you have something in mind for all of us. I'm not sure how to go about finding what that something is. How will you go about revealing yourself to us? Is it my fault that I haven't found you yet because I have taken you for granted or not been open enough? I will continue searching—but when will I know?

The entire world
is closing in on me

Dear God,

Please send help; I need it
desperately. I feel as though the entire
world is closing in on me. School is such
a bitch, I can't seem to get a break from
anyone. There is nothing but pressure
everyplace. Everyone wants me to make a
different decision and none of them are
the one I want to make. Give me guts
enough to do what I think is right, and
help it to be a decision that is right. Also
make me man enough to accept the
results of these decisions.

A loving and protecting father

Father,

I'm sorry that I haven't talked much to you before, but I just wanted to let you know that I know you are always present and willing to help. I wish I had more time to talk, but I'm a daydreamer. Since I'm growing up and my attitudes about life are changing, I don't really know who I am. The only way I can really be at peace with myself is to take a walk in the woods. That way I can be with simplicity and enjoy nature. I know that different people have different feelings about who you are; I'd like you to know who I believe you are. To me, you seem like a loving and protecting father who is always ready to help us (your children) when we need it. Thanks!

Your daughter

P.S. Please be patient with me because even if I don't talk much to you, I still love you and I know that you love me.

Will I be me?

God,

What's going to become of me? Am I going to become what I expect of myself? Will I be a success in whatever I undertake for my life's work? Or will I be a failure in everything? Will I have a happy life that will be rich and fulfilling? Will I be me?

Why have I been so alone lately?

Dear God,

Why have I been so alone lately? I have felt like nobody cares. I know it must be me—it's not everybody else ignoring me. I'm constantly feeling sorry for myself. Could it be you just trying to get into my life?

I don't know anybody as well as I want to and I don't know what to say when I think I'm getting close to someone.

God, forgive me for not appreciating the beauty you surround me with.

Help me appreciate everyone that I come into contact with, especially myself.

There is
an emptiness present

Dear God,

How do I know what is expected out of me in life? I try to talk to you, but I never seem to find the answers. I try to thank you, but there is an emptiness present. Yet I feel that you are there. It's just a feeling, but I guess that gives me reason to keep searching for you. I see you most when I look up in the sky on a nice clear night and see all the stars and say to myself, "There's got to be someone greater than man; there's got to be a God."

Someday, maybe,
I will find you

Dear God,

I hope you know I'm searching for you. You are really hard to find. Sometimes, however, I find you at my darkest times. Thanks for being there at those times. I want you to know that when the situation gets tough, I'll be looking. Someday, maybe, I will find you. I'll always be looking.

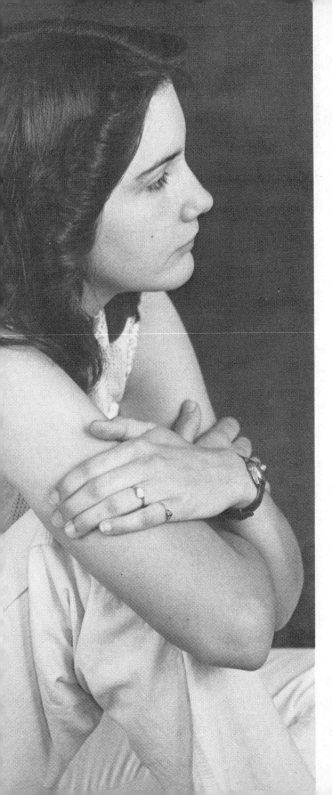

Have you disappeared?

God,

Who are you? What is your purpose? Why does everybody put more emphasis on you than on anything else? We are all taught to love and have faith in you, and that you will protect us. But where are you when we need help the most? Have you disappeared and are you hiding from me? I hope that someday I can have the strength to really believe that you will love and protect me. Please help me in doing that.

Sincerely,

Hopeful

God,
this is a year of decision

God,

    This is a year of decision and I need
you to help me. There were many times I
doubted you existed and I didn't even
think you knew me. But you do know me;
you're in my life everyday and I need you
now more than ever. Forgive me for
taking so long to come to believe in you. I
need to feel secure, to know I'm making
the right decisions. Without you there,
God, it's impossible.

    I'm getting to be a woman now and I
like that feeling. But at times I'm so
unsure and I feel like a scared little girl. I
don't want to be a little girl anymore—I
want to grow to my fullest and be a
woman. I want to love and give love to
everyone so much right now. Right this
minute I could burst with happiness
because I feel you with me. Please stay
and never let this feeling go away.

A 17-year-old

Dear God,

Here I am doing something I expect a first grader to be doing—writing a letter to you. It sounds queer: a 17-year-old writing a letter like this. But maybe deep down inside me I am a first grader. I'm jealous of a lot of things: I always want recognition and I can be very two-faced at times. If I really was a 17-year-old, then maybe I would be a better person. I am just beginning to realize that I can't go through life without your help. I need you and my friends to help make me the 17-year-old that I should be and not the first grader that I am inside.

I open to you or whatever is love

Dear God . . .

I open to you or to whatever is love
Like a water lily on its course down
   a swirling curdling river,
Trying to bloom
Or like a dove,
   nestling down in a cool,
   abandoned wind-haunted eve,
   with more than a simple shiver.

What is being lonely?
Why is there such a thing as
   loneliness?
If all the lilies floating with me were
   to bloom,
   we might slow down that
   treacherous river a little.

Suggestions for Discussion and Dialogue

Perhaps you're reading this book by yourself, or perhaps you're part of a group that's going through these letters together. Whichever kind of person you are, the exercises below might help you get a better grasp on what the authors of the letters are trying to say. They might also lead you to some new discoveries about who you are. Try them out for yourself and see where they take you.

Think about some people with whom you would like to share these exercises: a close friend, your parents, your teenager, someone at school, someone at work. You might see your friendship deepen and a unique closeness start to happen — all because you were willing to entrust something of yourself to another.

Exercise 1
Write down your answers to the following questions. Remember, this is not an exam; what counts is simply expressing the way you feel.

1) Which letter in this section struck you the most? Why?

2) If you could say something to the author of that letter, what would it be?

3) How do the people who wrote the letters in this section seem to feel about God?

4) Many of these letters express uncertainty about God or questions about the purpose of life itself. Have you, in your life, ever felt the same way? Describe what that feeling or experience was like for you.

Exercise 2
Write a letter to God of your own. In this letter, tell him how you feel about him in your life right now. It doesn't have to be a long letter; the spelling and grammar don't have to be perfect. Just speak to the Lord from your heart.

How long, O Lord?
  Will you utterly forget me?
How long will you hide
  your face from me?
How long shall I harbor sorrow
  in my soul,
    grief in my heart
    day after day?
How long will my enemy
  triumph over me?

Psalm 13:2-3

II. Doubt and Suffering

At first glance, many of these letters will seem similar to those collected in Section I. What distinguishes these writings from those concerned with the search for purpose is the tone of of anguish, despair and pain which enters into the dialogue with God. The authors still search but with diminishing hope of finding the elusive Creator.

The reader may find echoes here of Job's argument with God: The evil and suffering of the world sear the heart; they seem omnipotent. It is not an abstract evil these authors write about. Rather, what emerges in these pages is personal tragedy, loss, death, loneliness.

In the face of such pain, the Church appears nothing but meaningless ritual and hypocritical congregations. Organized religion, for many of these writers, seems irrelevant at best—why bother with Church or even with God?

I find these letters difficult to read. I want to argue with the authors or point out God's love and the goodness of the world. If I am honest with myself, however, I know that I have felt these same ways many times before; and I recall my own struggles, never easy, with evil and suffering in my own life. I know also that I will undoubtedly question, complain, and argue with God again if I choose to be in a genuine relationship with him.

Sure,
you have problems too

Hey God,

Are you really up there? How come you never show yourself? Are you too ashamed of us? Sure, I know that we have real problems, which we created. Sure, we have to work them out. But don't you think that you could give us a hand?

We've tried and are trying our best, but most of it is not working. So, since you made us, why don't you help us instead of staying wherever you are and just looking down on us? Sure, you have problems too; but we should be your main concern, since you are our Father.

I personally can't complain, though, because you have given me a lot, and for this I am forever grateful. Thanks. It's not me I'm worried about, it's the rest of the world. Without some help from you, it will not work—I'm afraid we will cease to exist. So give us a break and consider it—please!

I don't care about you

Dear God,

    I don't really believe in you. I've gotten by without you for almost 18 years. I've been through death and crisis and still got by without you. I don't care about you. I care about me. I care about the people I love. I care about people.

    I am really a sensitive person and I am touched deeply very easily. I never talk to anyone about this but myself. I keep it all in, and that makes me a "Jesus" in my own way.

    I will never hurt a fellow person out of malice, although I have been crushed by other people's malice. I have loved and been loved and made love, and through it all I have never thought of you as my God. I have only one request of you, if you are really around. Have pity on my soul.

I am very doubtful of your existence

Dear God,

    This is a letter to tell you that I am very doubtful of your existence. However, don't let that bother you because I still believe in all of Jesus' teachings and morals concerning the love and respect each man owes his fellow man and himself. And if someday, through some experience, you reveal your existence to me, I think that it would help me to live a more confident life.

A force
binding all living things

Dear God,

I don't believe in you as one single being or a three-way divinity-thing either. I look at you as a supernatural force or power coexisting in harmony with the being of the universe. I don't believe you would single out this small planet in the vastness of space as your child, but I think you spread your force throughout the galaxy coexisting as a supernatural force binding all living things.

What's wrong with the woods?

To whom it may concern,

Why is it that people go to a building called a church when they really don't feel like being there? Who are they trying to impress — me, you, others? What's wrong with going outside in the woods or someplace like that? I mean, that is really your house, isn't it? Make others come to you; you don't have to come to them in a church. They built it expecting you to be there. I'd rather look at something you made, like nature, than look at four walls, which limit you.

Meditating

God:

I haven't been to church in a long time. Myself, I don't believe church helps me. But I do believe in you. I do pray in my own way. People would think I'm crazy if I told them how I prayed. I don't kneel or anything like that. I just sit and stare. I've had people say that it looks like I'm high. But I'm not. I call it meditating. I let my mind go blank, far away from the things around me. I recall the things I've done or haven't done or shouldn't have done. I try to find ways to better myself and to help people (which I've done a lot). I call this praying, and I think it does me a lot better than going to church. It helps me overcome obstacles in my life.

I have mixed feelings about your existence

I have mixed feelings about your existence. I try to believe that you're there, but at times it's very hard. It's all those times when things are going wrong that I really question myself about your existence. If I take a deeper look at my thinking, I realize that, even when things are going fine, I still forget to think about you and thank you. I don't pray; I guess I never really got into the habit.

I try to believe. But it's hard—damn hard.

To whom it may concern

To whom it may concern:

I don't have any philosophical questions for you concerning who I am or my eternal destiny.

I know who I physically am and what I aspire to be.

I am not concerned with the after-life, simply because I don't concern myself with death.

My world is concerned with the physical, concrete objects that I either now possess or will possess.

That is why I addressed this letter to "To whom it may concern," because at this point in time, religion and a god are not having such a great effect on me. That is not to say that they never could or will.

I may not be the holiest person

God:

I realize I may not be the holiest person in this world, and I don't try as hard as I should. It is tough to follow all the Christian ideals in this world of the teenager today. To tell you the truth, I don't know of too many people who are into your teachings. It just doesn't seem like the thing to do in today's world as far as the teenager goes. There must be sometime when we realize it. I'm just curious to find out when.

How can you let certain people suffer?

I'm really confused at times about you. I can't see how you can let certain people who have come into my life suffer the way they have. At times I find myself wondering if there is a God at all. It scares me a lot also; because deep down I believe and I don't know why I am thinking like this.

Do you bother to notice?

Dear God,

Well, I'm sorry I haven't heard from you in awhile. I can't tell really if it's my fault or yours, but we sure aren't as close to each other as we used to be.

For some time I've been told about how much you cared for me. I really liked the idea; it was kind of nice always having a person like you right at hand to talk to.

But over the last year or so I've really begun to wonder if you could care less. It began, I'll admit, with little things that never seemed to go right. Petty things they were, it's true. But after last Chrstmas I wonder even if you bother to notice what's going on down here—you know what I'm talking about. I prayed and prayed, but you still let the thing happen. It wasn't even a selfish prayer; I was praying for others, those I love. Yet you didn't seem to care. I've become very disillusioned.

I will continue to try to do the things that you wish. I want to thank you for all the wonderful things you have given me; I'm very lucky. I hope someday we can get back together again.

Yours truly . . .

So many doubts about myself

Dear God,

I don't know where I am right now. I don't believe in myself enough to have the confidence that others have in me. There are so many doubts about myself. Why don't people like me and why is it that I'm not important enough to be listened to? People are so occupied with themselves that they don't have time for me. It's not their fault, because they don't realize it; but what can I do to make them realize it? I love people and need their love and respect also.

I need some answers

Dear God,

Why do I suffer?
Why should I die?
Why do I lose my loved ones?
What good is it to hate someone?
Why is evil so tempting?
What is the reason for injustice?
Why can I not see your influence in the world?

These are the questions. I need some answers.

It just doesn't seem right

Dear God,

Where are you? I know you are supposed to be everywhere, but there are times when I just can't seem to find you. I see good and honest people getting hurt and dying. I see people who don't have enough to eat. Are you there with them? It just doesn't seem fair that people should have to suffer like that. I know that you suffered and died on the cross for us, and maybe I'm a little selfish, but it just doesn't seem right.

There are times when I really need someone, and I want to reach out, but I don't really know if you are listening. How can I learn to hear you better? What am I expected to do and become? I want to be able to do the right thing!

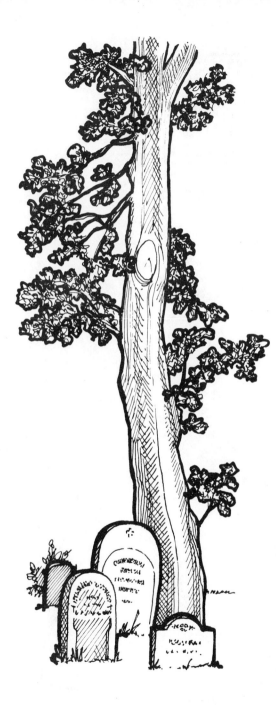

We don't take the time

Dear God,

A lot of things have happened to me in these past two months. Three people who meant something to me have died. I miss them a lot, of course; and at times I am even mad at you for taking them away from me. But then I realize that you loved them just as much as I did and you also wanted to be near them. I know I shouldn't be mad at you, but I guess it's just a human feeling or emotion you gave us.

Sometimes we neglect to take the time to go and really get involved with someone, either because we don't have the time or we really don't care. We don't take the time to talk, listen, or have a good time with them. But after they're gone, we suddenly realize that we never said, "I love you," or just, "You're really neat."

Now that they're gone, I wish I had told them. So, God, will you please say hi to them and, uh, send them my love.

Thanks,

An admirer

P.S. Help me to tell others while they're still here that I love them, maybe not just in words but in actions also.

You let my aunt die

Dear God,

Sometimes I can't understand some of the things you do. The past couple of years have been quite awful. You let my aunt die; she was only 40. Then my grandmother died, and she was the greatest. I know you wanted them to be with you, but I loved both of them very much. And I can't believe you did this. I know we all must die, but I didn't want them to die so soon. Death is always sad and people sometimes turn against you. But I never will. I know that I'm not an angel and I don't always go to church, but please don't hold it against me.

I want to ask you another favor. When you do decide to take my grandpa, please let him die peacefully. He's just barely living now and you're keeping him going. Thank you for that. You really do wonders.

Thank you for everything! You're beautiful.

Why can't one day go by

Dear Lord,

Why?

It seems like I can't go through just one day without hurting someone or being hurt myself. I know it's not right for me to ask questions. This is something that can't be changed so I should be willing to accept this. But it just doesn't seem fair! Why can't one day go by without seeing someone crushed, depressed, feeling left out?

Help me, Lord. Help me to do everything I can to avoid doing anything that would negatively affect anyone I'm close to. Please—help!

Thank you . . .

Flaws in people

God the Almighty
Paradise
Heaven (I forget the zip)

Dear God,

You'll have to forgive me for being so inquisitive. Why haven't you shown yourself in the last 2000 years? I ponder why a God so loving as you, a God who is love, can allow such things as death, hate, poverty, sickness, disappointment; drugs, wars, etc. to exist. Don't get me wrong—I don't blame you.

These problems are created by flaws in people—but people are created by you. Well, I've got to go now.

Your friend and (of course) mine . . .

When someone
very young dies

Dear God,

*I'm always wondering one thing:
Why is death always so painful and
unfair to us? I know it's supposed to be
the beginning of a beautiful life, but when
a young child or just someone very young
dies, it doesn't seem fair for them to die.
I guess I just don't understand death very
well.*

*Also, why do I sometimes wish I
were dead and never on this earth?
Sometimes I just want to quit everything.
I might be selfish to the people who love
me, but sometimes I even wonder if
anyone really does care.*

Why the absurdity?

Dear God,

*Why the absurdity? Why not reveal
yourself? Is this letter written to
nothing? I search for meaning like every
man. Are you the meaning? Are you
real?*

People say they believe in you and yet...

Dear God,

I wish I could believe in you. Sometimes it's so hard. I see all the bad things in the world and I find it hard to believe that with all this, something good can come out of it. People say they believe in you and yet they kill, hate, cheat, are prejudiced, and murder each other. They go to church every Sunday and act as pious as hell and put money in the basket and I hear them talk about "those damn niggers."

There's a lot of good things in this world, and for those I thank you (if you're there); but there are so many bad things. Why? Does anybody care? Show me that you do. Help me believe and act like I believe.

Thank you, God. I feel already that this letter has helped me. I just want to finish by saying, as the song goes, give me faith and hope and love and life. Please. I thank you, God. It's been good writing to you.

It's like playing
a card game

Dear God,

> *I feel I know you,*
> *but it's like playing a card game—*
> *this might be a bluff.*
> *So I need a sign*
> *to know that my believing in you*
> *is the right thing to do.*

Since I have been through it, I understand

God,

Everything you created is so beautiful. I sit here and look at all these wonderful people, each so different and so unique—you are so great and so good, the perfect person.

Yet sometimes you work in mysterious ways: loved ones die; babies die at birth; just when you are getting to know someone, something happens; people endure so much pain. But suddenly, since I have been through it, I understand a little more that it is for strength, for faith. Life can't always be perfect. Through your love, we can make it. We can learn to make the most of the hard times as well as the beautiful moments. All it takes is love and trust— for one another and for you.

I don't ever blame you

Dear God,

What I want to say is hard to put into words. I am a very strong believer in you and I always will be. Some people, when they are hurt by somebody or are not accepted by people, always ask the question, "Why is God doing this to me? Why is God letting me be hurt?"

But I don't, because I don't blame my being hurt on you, like other people do. I feel the world is to blame for having people who could hurt a person. I don't ever blame you for problems or the way people act. You would never do that, I think, to the people you created and love so much. I feel that people blame you because they are so hurt. You created every one of us, but you didn't make the way we act when we hurt someone. You always wanted us to love and give to everyone, so why should you do things to hurt us?

Suggestions for Discussion and Dialogue

As you work through the exercises following each section of letters, perhaps you would like to start gathering all of *your* letters and reflections into some kind of journal. Such a journal can become a map of your own journey to self-awareness and a deeper relationship with the Lord.

Exercise 3
Write down brief answers to the following questions:

1) Was there any letter in this section that summed up the way *you* feel about the world? Why?

2) Many of the letters in this section express anger at God and a deep doubt that he really cares about us, or even exists. How does it make you feel when you hear those doubts expressed?

3) What image of God comes out most strongly in these letters? (Examples: God as judge, as father, as distant, as friend, etc.)

4) What would you like to say in response to any one of the letters in this section?

Exercise 4
Write a letter to God in which you tell him about the way you feel concerning the problem of evil, suffering and injustice in the world. Be attentive to what he may be telling you in response.

Behold,
how good it is,
and how pleasant,
where brethren dwell at one!

Psalm 133:1

III. Relationships: Love and Loneliness

Relationships with other people perform an important function in enabling our identity to take shape. Teenagers discover much about themselves by interacting with family, peers and members of the opposite sex. They recognize, perhaps for the first time, their uniqueness, giftedness and lovableness because of friendships and love relationships. Commitment and self-sacrificing concern usually occur later in life; what characterizes adolescent relationships is this process of growing self-awareness and identity.

The letters in this section express the multitude of feelings which arise because of relationships. There is concern or anger that one is not trusted by one's parents; there is the insecurity of not knowing what one's friends think; there is the loneliness of isolation or rejection; and there is the overflowing joy of having a "special person" in one's life.

God is seen here as someone particularly concerned with relationships. The connection keeps being made between God and treating other people with compassion and love. Something of the Good News that "God is love" seems to have taken root in the consciousness of these authors.

In this period
of being turned off

Well, this is as good a way as I can
think of to start a letter that I don't know
how to begin.

There is so much to question or
reason out. In this period of being turned
off, is it me? What am I doing that is
sending people away from me instead of
closer? Do others feel that I'm being a
bitch, or what? All of a sudden, they will
hardly talk to me. Or is it me? Am I
making them seem less than they are, or
am I treating them the same way?
Sometimes I don't know, other times I
don't care.

I get tired of trying to make people
like me when I get no return response. I
realize that isn't what I should be after,
but without it I feel I'm pushing myself on
people . . .

Why am I so suspicious?

Oh God, why am I like I am? Why am I so suspicious of my friends' actions? Is it because I'm afraid, so insecure? What am I to do? When I'm with a group of people, some of us always argue. Why can't we be peaceful and happy, Lord? We don't seem to realize that we may not have tomorrow — that is in your hands. Help us to be more understanding with each other and to show our love now while we still have it.

It is through my friends and family that I find you — through their thoughtfulness, kindness and love — and yes, even through their anger. Thank you, Lord, for these people that have helped me to find you, and I pray that I'll never lose them. Please bless us, Lord, and help us to be the peaceful, loving people you want us to be!

Are they really my friends?

Dear God,

Where do I go from here? How do I find what I am really like? Where, here on earth, do I have to go to find the answers? Am I looking in the right places?

The people I spend most of my time with — are they really my friends, or just people who laugh behind my back? Do they really know how I feel, or do they just play along like they do?

Why is it that the people who seem to mean the most to me are taken away from me when I just find how much they can help me find myself?

Do I want to get serious, or do I want to run away from any kind of relationship like that?

God, you know me so well. Why don't I understand and know you as well? You have yourself put together, while I seem to fall apart. Here I am, knowing that I care inside, but not knowing what to care for. It seems that if I begin to care for something, it leaves. Why? Help me put my head together. When I love someone, give me the strength to know that that person may reject my feelings totally.

Help me keep everything straight in my path of life. Lead me in my path to growing up.

My parents don't love each other anymore

Dear God,

   I would like to thank you for all the wonderful things you have given me.
   But there is just one thing I don't understand. It says in the Bible that parents are supposed to love each other until death. Well, then, why is it that my parents don't love each other anymore? Do you think maybe if you and I worked together we could bring back that love between them? I think between the two of us we can make it happen for them again. I'm willing to give it a try if you are.
   Oh, I want to thank you for that special person you brought into my life. You know who he is. I just wish I could be with him all the time, but at least I know he's there and he cares!

How come
mom doesn't trust me?

Dear God,

I would like to tell you what's going on in my life, but for some reason I think you know.

The first thing I'd like to ask of you in my letter is this: How come Mom doesn't trust me? She knows I'm really a good kid and wouldn't do anything wrong, but there is always that, "Well, where does he live?" "Make sure you're in by one o'clock, 'cause I'll be waiting," etc. I know Mom and Dad really love me and are just doing it for my good (or something of that sort!), but I just can't take it. If you could help in any way, it would make me happy.

And oh, God, why can't you make me and my brother get along better?

If you do have time to answer my letter, fill me in on the exciting future ahead of me. And if you want to, you can give me some tips I might need.

Love you . . .

We were so close

Dear God,

I need help to understand why things happen. Some things make no sense.

I feel that my best friends and I are becoming farther and farther apart. It bothers me very much, because we were so close and shared so many things. Please let us be more understanding of each other and don't let popularity be the reason we don't want to be around each other. That is so unimportant—let us be less selfish.

There are so many other things that are more important than ourselves. I wish we could all realize that.

I just wish
we could talk together

Dear God,

   *I wish that my mother and I could
be a little bit closer. Our family is close,
yet we don't really confide in each other
or tell anyone our hopes, aspirations, or
heartfelt disappointments or sorrows.*

   *My mother and I don't always
exactly see eye-to-eye. I can pretty much
see her point of view, but I wish she could
see mine, or even just ask for my opinion.
Maybe I don't act or look like I want to
talk to her. I love her very much and I
know that she loves me. I just wish we
could talk together over general things
and more personal opinions and ideals.*

I'm so lost

Dear God,

   *First of all, thank you so very much
for all that you have given to me: my
parents, friends, etc. I need so much
help, though; I'm so lost. I smoke dope—
too much, I know. But really, in a way, I
have to, just to help me forget what kind
of person I've been, how I take advantage
of all the things you have given me.*

   *I'm really disappointed with most of
the male race. They take too much
advantage of me—they all use me. All
they want or look for is sex. They all
want it when we start the relationship,
when I really like them. Then, when they
start liking me, I don't like them
anymore. I wish I was still a virgin for the
man who will someday really love me. I
love you. I wish you were here now to
help.*

   *I think the contrast between my
parents and me is too much. I think
sometimes I'm going crazy. I love my
parents, but why can't they understand
why I can't talk about having sex or
smoking pot? Nobody will listen,
because they don't want to help. They
just are so against everything I do. But if
they would help me, I wouldn't do it. I
need someone . . .*

Give me a different high

Dear God, Jesus Christ,

Maybe it's just that I don't give enough time to you, but I really don't know what to do with my girlfriend. I think I really love her and I want to go to bed with her. Maybe it's all wrong, but I feel it's all right in my eyes. I really wish you would come into my life and give me a different high than pills and pot. I know that my life would be a hell of a lot better if you guided my life.

I don't know what to say to her. I just don't know. I really want to help her; I really love and care for her. She is one beautiful person. The problem is, she keeps her feelings locked up inside her and she has to get them out, but she can't. She's not the type of person to let her feelings out. If only you can help me know what to do.

The gift of
being able to open up

Dear God,

I feel as if for the first time in a long
while I have opened up to someone else.
Opening up really isn't as difficult as I've
always feared. A weight has been lifted
off of me. I now cherish the gift of being
able to open up every now and then. It
makes me wonder why people are so
afraid of one another. Why do people
hide behind masks? Why do people care
so much about what others think? In this
computerized society, the only way you
can stay sane is by being an individual. If
we all try to act the same, where will it
lead?

I can tell him
my joys and sorrows

God,

I want to thank you for the friend
you've sent me! He's very special and he
makes me feel very special. I can talk to
him, tell him my joys and sorrows, my
hopes and fears. We're planning on
getting married in a couple of years, and
we'll be calling on you together for help
as we encounter problems.

Thank you for him, my family, and
most of all, life.

Your presence in other people

Universal Mind,

I really don't seem to know you, yet I feel your presence in other people. Each person seems so unique, yet each holds a friendly tone and grace when they lose the defenses they have. You know, it seems funny that I have such a person, who really sticks out to me as a real person. Other people don't seem to tell me the truth, but when I talk to my dear one I feel that she is really truthful to me and that I can feel a real bond of love with this person. I hope I can always feel this radiation from her and from other people. The radiation of being open and friendly and honest — a faith in being a person.

Suggestions for Discussion and Dialogue

Since the letters in this section deal with relationships and friendships, try to share the answers to these questions with a friend. Be aware of any hesitations or fears you may have about doing this. What is it that holds you back? It might even be worthwhile to bring those feelings to God and to ask him for *freedom*.

Exercise 5
Write down brief answers to the following questions:

1) Which letter in this section made the strongest impression on you? Why?

2) Several of the authors talk about finding God through other people—family, boyfriend or girlfriend, best friend. What does this mean to you in your life?

3) Remember a time when you experienced negative feelings about a relationship—loneliness, anger, jealousy. Describe what that was like for you and how you handled those feelings.

4) Write down the names of your closest friends. Now, next to each name, write down one quality that really makes that person special to you.

Exercise 6
Write a letter to God in which you describe one important relationship in your life right now. Perhaps it is a relationship that makes you very happy, or perhaps it is one in which there are some difficulties or misunderstandings. Whatever kind of relationship it is, bring it to God in this letter. Describe your feelings about it to him, remembering that he will listen to whatever you have to say.

When I call, answer me,
O my just God,
you who relieve me
when I am in distress;
Have pity on me,
and hear my prayer!

Psalm 4:2

IV. Petitions

What is striking about the petitions in this section is that, for the most part, the requests concern *general* rather than *specific* situations. Even in those letters which detail a person's life or need, the authors almost always sum up their prayer with a petition dealing with inner realities. God is asked to grant patience, hope, the ability to love, strength to grow into responsible adulthood.

Many of the letters are cries out of the depths, asking much more for relationship than for material goods. The ability to articulate these needs indicates the presence of both hope and trust.

A good communication level with God

If I were writing a letter to God, I would ask him to give me the faith to believe in him and keep that faith in good and bad times. Also, to help shape me into the type of person who wasn't overly religious but who was a good person. Also, to make me the type of person that was conscious of his sinful faults and, most of all, to give me the strength needed to overcome them. Also, to help me overcome prejudices and to help me to come to respect my parents. To help me have some real meaning in life and to understand really what life's all about.

To help me be a mature person, not selfish, since all God really asks of us is to be good Christians. All in all, I would like to be on a good communication level with God and to be on that level for the rest of my life.

Help us
make the right decisions

Jesus:

    Guide me and all of us into the future. Send us a light which we can follow. Help us to make the right decisions. Don't give up on us when we annoy you with sin and hate. Though we don't always show you our outward appreciation, we all love you.

Let me know
I am not alone

Dear God,

    Knowing you are alive and aware around us, I'd like some direction that would be helpful in these "hard" times. Not a sign or revelation, but some acknowledgement that I made the right choice. School's hard, family life can be straining at times, friends can turn away for a time, so some guidance through this mess would help me to find my weaknesses that may be the cause for some of these problems. It is mainly up to me, but encouragement from you would let me know I am not alone.

I need you
in everything I do

Dear Lord,

I need you in everything I do, so help me, Lord, to be more like you and to be a better Christian. Lord, help my parents to understand me, and to look at my side of things and not always theirs. And help them to understand that I am old enough to make my own decisions. Help me to stay away from all temptation. Help my relationship with my boyfriend to grow stronger only if it is your will, Lord. Help me to know what you want and expect of me during my life-time, what my role is in life. Lord, help me to get to know you better and get to know others better. Lord, thanks for listening. Remember that I love you, Lord, and I know you feel the same toward me. Thanks again.

This problem
I just can't drop

Dear God,

Even though I am a sinner, I still love you. As you know, I have a problem, which I will not put into this letter because I am very ashamed of this fault. I'm asking you with all sincerity to help me overcome this problem. I feel that it will hurt me in my future life. God, I'm really not that bad, but I just can't drop this problem. I've tried many times to quit it, but couldn't. If in any way or form you can help me, please do, dear God. I love you more than anything else in the universe and I love my parents more than anything else in this world.
Please help me, God.
Thank you.

Love you . . .

Wasn't it easier when my parents were young?

Dear God,

*Why am I so unsure of who I am?
Wasn't it easier when my parents were
young and the superficial rules were
spelled out for them? Now I have to
make so many decisions. Help me choose
the right course or at least make me feel
sure of my choice. Help me keep from not
deciding at all, because that is the worst
thing possible.*

To use the talent
you gave me

Dear God,

   You know me. You know my
weaknesses and my strong points. Please
help me to correct these weaknesses, and
also to appreciate the love that I'm so
fortunate to share with many people.
Help me find a sense of direction in my
life and to use the talent you gave me in a
positive way that will help others.

Help me see
through the faults

Dear God,

   I'd like to ask you a favor. I'd like
you to help me help myself and to help
me see through the faults of other people
and let them see through my faults.

Not the stereotype teenager

I would like to ask God to help me with my feelings of insecurity in my life, by trying to help me be myself, to be open, and not to be the stereotype teenager who has to be popular and the class cutup. Also, help me when it comes to being able to relate in a serious way to other people. It seems like I put a mask on my feelings even though I know I should bring them out.

Help me not to be a fake

Hi God,

It seems stupid writing to you, as you know all that I can think, even before I do. But maybe through this letter I can better understand myself.

I really have nothing specific to talk about, but help me to be myself, to do what I do to the best of my abilities. Help me not to be a fake—not something my friends want me to be or think I am. Give me the strength to depart from the crowd, the strength to follow the path set by my heart. Also, help me to see what I really want, not something I think I want because everyone else wants it.

Thanks . . .

You,
the one with the big beard

Hey God (yeah, you, the one with the big beard and the white cloak),

I need help! The entire world is going by too fast and I can't keep up with it all. I have no time anymore to sit and think, to relax and enjoy life. It's a hassle here, a hurry there, and run off to the next place. Make the days 12 hours longer. Or, if you can't do that, teach me how to relax and how to cope with the pressures. Teach me how to enjoy your gifts, especially the people whom I love and who love me. Thanks—I owe you one.

This ton of bricks called adolescence

Dear God,

Keep it up; it's all down hill from here. Be at the stops along the way. I won't see you there, but help me to continue anyway. Head me in the right direction to the end of the line. Keep this ton of bricks called adolescence from breaking my back in two.

Bring us together

Dear God,

Bring us together.
With our own private lives and troubles, we seem to be separated.
Will you show me why I am here?
How should I live? What must I do before I die? Lord, bring love, dignity and understanding into our lives. Help our troubled times to be lighter. Help our sorrows to be few. Help us to be better and happier people.

Suggestions for Discussion and Dialogue

Answering these questions and writing these letters can be more than mere "exercises" for you. As you reflect and write and share, maybe you will find that this process becomes a genuine prayer of your own. Spend a few moments before you begin the following exercise to slow down, to listen to your breathing and to become aware that the Lord is very much with you right now.

Exercise 7
Write brief answers to these questions:

1) Did any of the letters in this section express something you might have said to God? How so?

2) What kinds of things do the authors of these letters seem to be asking God for?

3) Have you ever asked God for something you didn't receive? How did that affect your relationship with God?

4) Do you think any of your prayers have ever been answered? What were your feelings when you believed that God had actually heard you?

Exercise 8
Remember when Jesus said, "Ask, and you will receive" (Mt 7:7)? Do you believe that? Write a letter to God in which you ask him for something that's really important to you right now. Afterwards, don't forget you asked him; be on the alert for his answer.

Truly you have formed
   my inmost being;
   you knit me
   in my mother's womb
I give you thanks
   that I am fearfully,
   wonderfully made;
   wonderful are your works.

Psalm 139: 13-14a

V. Thanks and New Awareness

Of the 5,000 letters I have read and categorized, more than 40 percent have as their predominant theme a sense of thankfulness and gratitude toward God. Moreover, many letters whose chief theme would place them in another category include at least a sentence or paragraph expressing thanks. This fact has been an unexpected and striking discovery for me; frankly I would have expected the majority of letters to be of the "asking" variety.

Why does gratitude recur so often in these letters? I attribute this partially to the context in which the letters were written. In the course of a retreat at the Jesuit Renewal Center, we lead the students through a reflection on their life-journey from birth up to the present. Such a reflection becomes a meditation on the significant ways in which God has touched each individual through people and events. Furthermore, we spend a good bit of the retreat helping adolescents become more aware of their own goodness, of the gifts they've been given by God. An atmosphere is created in which they come to a renewed sense of awe and wonder at the mystery of life. They recognize what is of ultimate importance, what is truly valuable: friendship, love, nature, God. For those familiar with the *Spiritual Exercises* of St. Ignatius, these are the themes of the "Principle and Foundation."

The tone of these letters is reminiscent of love letters. Perhaps that is what they are, for one author even addresses God as "dearest lover and confidant." This section of the letters is characterized by a certain ingenuousness, at times almost a naivete. Although some of them are certainly flowery in style, the sincerity and intimacy expressed is without doubt genuine. They are psalms of praise.

Sky, earth and sea

God,

    I take for granted all that is around
me:
      sky, earth, and sea,
      things I see every day,
      friends and people I meet.
    I just want to say:
      Thank you, God,
      for letting me see all the
      wonderful things
      I take so casually
      and for making me realize how
      important and meaningful life
      can be.

God, I'm a miracle!

Dear God,

There is so much to thank you for. I can remember times when I was messing around with my friends, or at a basketball game, and all of a sudden I was kind of looking at myself from a distance and I'd think—God! I'm a miracle! I can see and touch and hear what I really hear. Dear God—I'm a miracle!

I want so many things in life—little things to ask for—but when I think of what you have already given me—all the things—I'm satisfied. Thank you for me. Thank you for my miracle and thank you for letting me share my miracle. I love you; I don't worship you. I can't worship anybody I really love. I love you for what you gave, what you do and what you are.

Me

A castle in the sky

Hi God!

You know what? I really want to be someone special. There are so many great things in life, but I'm uncertain as to which direction I'm going in. But wherever my life is leading me, I hope you realize that I'm depending on you to guide me and encourage me. Maybe I fall away from where I should be, but I'm trying.

Maybe you didn't notice, but last week there was a cloud shaped like a castle. It was beautiful. I looked up and suddenly I realized that it was there to cheer me. It's not the monotony of everyday life that keeps us going; otherwise we'd give up. No, it's the little things that keep us going—like a castle in the sky. You planned that for me, didn't you?

It's hard to say I love you; it's scary. But I do, God.

Your friend always . . .

I have seen you

Dear God,

> I have seen you in the early hours,
> In the silent sunrise behind the
>   breezy morning sea,
> In the grace of the gulls,
> In the smiles of the beach-walkers
>   holding hands.
> God, I have felt you in the warmth
>   of the sun,
> In the gentle spring breeze,
> Which lifts my surging spirit.
> I have felt you in me, not knowing
>   who it was.
> God, I have heard you in the owl's
>   call,
> In the baby's laugh, in cheerful
>   shouts.
> I have heard you in wise men's
>   voices
> Calling me to you.

Despite hard times

Dear God,

You know what suffering is; you have known pain. You know that such pain can fill our hearts. But you also give us the strength to make it through, to hold on, and the hope that a brighter day will come, a chance to know the love and happiness you offer us through others. And for this, God, despite hard times, we thank you.

The third planet has its drawbacks

Dear God,

Thank you for making earth so beautiful. I always feel closest to you when I look at your creations. Sometimes it's hard to imagine heaven as being even more lovely. The third planet has its drawbacks, of course, but it also has a lot of good points. I find you in nature. As I look at it, I see the infinite love and patience that you love to put into each tiny detail — the details that make up the whole. Thank you.

Signed,

Occupant

Spontaneous, casual

God,

I thank you for your friendship. At times I'm angry, confused, or frightened. Other times, I'm very happy and at ease. You're always beside me, like a friend, through good times and bad. I can't help but think of you in an informal way. To me you're not a mighty God in some far-away heaven, but instead you're a special friend, always present, always near. When I pray to you, it's spontaneous, casual. I can ask you for help, tell you about something that's happened, or just tell you how great I feel. Thanks.

When spring arrives

Dear God,

I love life. When spring arrives and all the flowers open up and the air is filled with sweet fragrance, I think of you. When I walk and see a mother with a small child, I see love, and I think of you. How great are all your creations!

I love love. When I see an elderly couple holding hands on a park bench, I think of you. When I see a white man shake the outstretched hand of a black man, I see love, and I think of you. How great is your love!

Even the animals know love. Cats nestle up in their owners' laps and horses nudge one another with their noses. Dogs wag their tails. When I see all of this, I think of you.

Young love, old love, brotherly love—love is life.

Thank you, God, for so many kinds of love. Thank you, God, for life!

Sincerely . . .

Thank you for caring

Hi,

Well it's me again. Yeah, I know the only time you hear from me is when I'm asking for something. But this time it's different. I'm thanking you for being around when I needed you. Hope you know my feelings because it's hard to put them into words. I just wanted to thank you for caring.

Thanks . . .

Above the sky was so gray

Dear God,

    I was out walking and we came to the edge of a cliff. Down below was the river, slowly moving, so green. Above, the sky was so gray, and all around us the trees were so bare. Then it started to snow softly. I was struck so very much by the beauty and peace surrounding me. I thank you for that moment and all the moments in the past and the future when you make yourself known to me and show me your love. Thank you, dear Lord, for everything.

                Your loving daughter

Bits and pieces of memories

Dearest God,

    Many times I sit back and wonder who you are and how much you mean to me. My life has been bits and pieces of memories, memories of good times and of bad. And when I try to put all of them together I have you, and that's a lot.

    In finding you, I grew closer to you. I see you everywhere: in my friends, family, love. I believe in you, yet I don't understand you, your feelings, your ways.

    I'm writing this letter to tell you something I guess I've never really come out and told you. I'm sorry it's been this way. Sometimes it's hardest to say the things that mean so much to you. Why is it that way? I guess what I really want to tell you is I love you. I'm sorry I never told you this before.

    In closing, I want to thank you for my friends. They mean everything in the world to me, God. Without friends, I don't know where I'd be. But most of all, God, I want to thank you for just letting me be me.

                Love,

                Me

I'll find my way to you

Dear God,

I don't know how to tell you how I feel. You know everything anyway. I hope you know I love you even if I don't live like your son. It's hard sometimes to decide between you and my friends. It's really hard to put you into my life without feeling like a religious fanatic. I know you love me and, God, I really try to love you, too. I know you're always there for me. Please don't be upset if I don't look your way. It's hard for me.

I just want to say thanks, I guess. You've always been there for me and I feel safe knowing that. And I know you're always trying to let me find my own way to you. I really don't see how you put up with me at times. I just want to let you know that when I do things you don't like, it's not to go against your word or anything; it's usually because I get confused. It's my way of asking for help. I'm glad when you're there to give it to me.

Don't worry, I'll find my way to you. I have to. I know you. I couldn't live without your love and strength to guide me.

How much
I've taken for granted

Dear God,

*How much I've taken for granted!
Sometimes I just wish I had more time —
and then I look back and wish I'd used
the time you gave.*

*I wish I could hold people in my
embrace forever. They touch me, they
linger, and then are swiftly gone. I touch
my hand, remembering their soft, gentle
touch. I reach out again to return the love
I feel — but it is too late. They are never
to feel the kisses, the tears, my hand that
wants to touch them. How I remember
yesterday, and so want to be there, to
relive those moments, and tell those
people how much I love them. Yet when
that yesterday was my today, I told
myself I would do it tomorrow. But
tomorrow came too soon, and yesterday
is gone.*

I was just always asking

Hey God!

*How are things going? Everything
here for the most part has gone well. This
year will probably be the most difficult of
all four years at _____ High. You'll
probably be hearing from me a lot,
because I know now that it is hard to get
along without you. Remember how I felt
not long ago, the feeling that you weren't
there? Maybe, now that I think about it, I
was just always asking and not really
giving anything in return. Or maybe you
were answering and I wasn't listening,
because what you were saying was not
exactly what I wanted to hear.*

Well, I'm sure glad that's over!

With your help
I can be freed

Dear Jesus,

What do I say to one who has given me so much? I feel so many things, it's hard to specify each one. I really want to thank you for my life here and the chances I've been given to share this life. But in the same breath, I want to ask your forgiveness for the countless opportunities I have missed.

Only recently have I been able to see your true simplicity and beauty, especially in the world you have created for us, your children. And only recently have I been able to believe you love me — me, relatively nothing by my own standards, but really something beautiful in your eyes. Through these realizations, I've finally been able to start to love and to weed out all that has been keeping me back from you and your love. There's still a lot of garbage surrounded by those brick walls, but I know that with your help I can be freed of all this because you're my friend, savior, helper and, best of all, my God. There is nothing else I should want. Thank you, Jesus.

A child of a king

A little bit of heaven
on earth

God,

I know you are with me and I feel safe. I see you everywhere because I believe you show a little bit of heaven on earth in all the beautiful moments I feel and see. I've just recently started really living, enjoying your earth and the people on it. Please help others to realize it, too, and open up to understanding and feeling. People are really beautiful. Help me be part of it all.

I owe you,
well, my life

Dear God,

This is me. You made me and I feel I owe you—well, my life. I am because of you. There are times when I have doubted you, but you stuck with me. There were times when you could have let me die, but you must have thought I was worth something, because I am still here. These few times have brought me closer to you. It's a shame I didn't come to you on my own. I am sorry. But thanks God for letting me be. I've got it good and today I'm realizing it.

Thanks again . . .

Friends are more important
than possessions

Dear God,

Thank you for giving me everything you have. At times I want more than I have. But then I have to realize: Why do I think I am so special? And that everything I want should be mine? Other people have less than me and are happier. Maybe I am too self-concerned; I want everything for me. Well, I think I realized today how much I really have. And I think that after today I will be more thankful because now I realize friends are more important than possessions. And you never know how long life will last. While a possession can last forever, a life can be very short. Too short sometimes. Thanks.

I never could find the intellectual answer

Dear God,

I remember going through a lot of questions about you in my life, but I never really could find the intellectual answer. It's not there. People have to trust their own hearts.

Sometimes I wonder if I'm copping out by not worrying if you exist — or even wondering, like some people do. I think people just have to decide if they want to believe or not. I don't think I would be happy without you. I don't think I would have anything to live for. I live for love, trying to improve my love for life and my love for people. That's what you're all about and I love you. As long as that's there, everything will be easy.

Thank you for letting me be here to write this. I've never done this before, Lord. In a way, this is better than praying. You feel like your thoughts are clearer or they mean more when you can write them down. I will have to take the time to do this more often. Thanks for listening. I believe you are.

Now I know
that I am not alone

Dear God,

   I don't know why I'm alive in this
world, but I do know that you gave me
life: a chance to live, to breathe, to love,
to feel the sun and wind, and to be loved
back. I came here confused, feeling alone
and very different from everyone else, but
now I know that I'm not alone. I've
learned how to open up, to understand
the feelings of others, and to realize that
I'm not so unique with my troubles. I
know you care for me, and I can feel you
around me — in me — everywhere, if I just
listen for a moment and pause. Because
you are always near, I don't worry so
much about my problems, and I have
more confidence and insight into myself
and those around me than ever before.
Thank you for caring, and thank you for
giving me a chance to live and experience
all of the things you've given us.

My love has no end

Dearest lover and confidant,

I have come to know that within myself there is much to rejoice in. I have come to a desire for your touch; I want to be so much, and I am unable to accomplish it without you. I proclaim this with my thoughts and, while I know its truth, I fear the desire yearning within me is not yet strong enough. I beg that you not let me lie sterile and alone for long— but I trust in you. I believe in you, I want to know you, understand you, feel you, and for you to know me, to touch my being and humanness.

Lend me your strength that I might strive to know my brothers and call them by the name of friend. Help me to overcome my fears, that I might try to love and understand and be a person worth the gift of life and love. I am striving for that end. "My love has no end and you are its beginning."

Love,

Me

I hear your whisper

My friend:

Without you I am nothing. I own nothing. Stop—think. I hear your whisper in quiet thought which some call prayer. I hear your voice when I least expect it. Be with me always. I have a bad tendency of shoving you into the back of my mind, when in reality you are the life-blood of my existence. Keep me growing. I can't stop now. Teach me to see you in the midst of my suffering, to believe in resurrection.

85

Suggestions for Discussion and Dialogue

To be grateful, as the authors of these letters obviously are, means that we have awakened and that we see the world and ourselves with fresh eyes. It means that we have broken out of habit and drudgery and that we want to celebrate. Take a moment now to let your anxiety and tension slip away; breathe deeply, and become aware that you are alive. Become aware that you are loved.

Exercise 9
Write brief answers to the following questions:

1) Which letter in this section attracted you the most? Why?

2) Write down some things or people in your life that you think you sometimes take for granted.

3) Has there been a time in your life recently when you found it difficult to be grateful to God? Describe the situation and your feelings about it.

4) How do you think you would go about keeping alive a spirit of thankfulness in your life from day to day?

Exercise 10
Go back in memory through your life and recall moments when you were happy, times you felt loved, periods when you felt really alive. Write a letter to God in which you try to put into words what you are thankful about in your life up to this moment.

But God has heard;
he has hearkened
to the sound of my prayer.

Psalm 66:19

VI. Dialogues With God

When we write down what we think God would say to us in a letter, our image of God—how we perceive him—becomes quite clear. In the letters *from* God in this final section, some of the authors obviously perceive God as something of a judge, a moral teacher who sternly wags his finger at the erring student. One writer imagines God warning him to "use your time wisely." Another author, half-humorously, has God admonishing her to "lay off the chocolate and greasy foods." In other letters, however, God is revealed as someone of great compassion and gentleness. He reassures the authors they are loved. He encourages them to trust their own goodness. He urges them to be less anxious about the future and less preoccupied with death.

From one point of view, these letters from God are the voices of the authors' own inner wisdom. But to put it another way, they are the articulation of the Spirit's own voice, the Spirit of God who dwells within our heart of hearts.

Thank you for your thought-provoking letter

Dear God,

Thank you for allowing me to have a good life. I realize that I haven't really gotten into it because I'm only 16. I hope that when I grow up and have a family, if I do, that it will be as good and healthy and together and nice as mine is now. I think I have a good start. Thanks for everything you've given me.

From a faithful
admirer

Dear Faithful Admirer,

Thank you for your thought-provoking letter. I'm glad you like the way your life has been going. I've scheduled many exciting events for the coming years.

Sometimes it's nice to think about the future, but other times it's better to take life as it comes.

Signed,

XXX

God

Nobody knows
the exact time

Dear God,

 Thank you for my girl. Help me figure out problems that might arise between us, so we can get through them and still remain good friends.

 Thank you for a great family life and relationship with my family. Thank you for understanding and trusting parents.

 Thank you not so much for the good times I've had, but the good times you've let me help someone else have—which they might not have had otherwise.

 Mostly thanks for making my family and friends happy.

Dear ___,

 About your letter: You're welcome for the things you thanked me for: your girlfriend, parents, health, good times, helping people have good times.

 But remember: Use your time wisely, for nobody knows the exact time or hour when this will all come to an end.

 Yes, after life it will be beautiful, but it will not be beauty you can understand now, so use your time wisely.

 Don't be selfish.

Try letting other people into your life

Dear God,

Hi. It's me again. You know, I feel like I'm writing to Santa Claus. I guess because you're somebody not seen, but believed in by a lot of people; and you do nice things for people. I am lying in front of these flowers and they remind me of the ones I bought for my mom on Christmas Eve. The reason I keep relating to Christmas is because I'm happy.

I'm a person with and without a lot of things. Although I am without some of the finer things, there is still somebody who loves me very much. One of those somebodies is a guy I have been going with for almost a year. Although he doesn't drive and have a job—that's usually what most guys have and they supply transportation and nice things for a girl—he supplies the love I need as me. And I guess I do fine for him. Thank you, Lord, for this and my family.

I love you,

Me

P.S. When are you going to clear up my face?

Dear ___,

I love you. I only wish you'd stop long enough to listen and consider what I and other people are trying to say to you. Try letting other people into your life. I am glad I could be of some help as far as your love from your family and boyfriend. Why don't you, in return, pass out some of that love?

Love,

God

P.S. I will clear up your face when you meet me half-way. Like, lay off the chocolates and greasy foods.

Hang in there
and just believe

Dear God,

Answer a question for me. How does a person know if he has a strong faith? Or how is a person supposed to know if he is doing as you asked of us? It seems that you're just there, as we have learned in elementary school, and we just believe that. Well, I guess that's what faith's all about: belief. I wish you would have given us more to go on — maybe some kind of fact. An answer would reassure my faith for sure.

Thanks,

Anonymous

Dear Anonymous,

Thank you for writing such an interesting letter about your faith problem — about wanting some facts about faith for some kind of proof. Well, it's hard to put into fact, so hang in there and just be a believer, because a strong believer has strong faith. And that is what is so neat about my world. Fact doesn't stop any one person from believing or make them stop having faith.

J.C.

This is why
I have created you

Dear Lord,

Hi! What have you been doing lately? Created any new galaxies?

I'm having a hard time writing this to you. I've never written a letter to the creator of all things before. It's really a weird feeling to think that you'll receive this. For simplicity's sake, may I refer to you as "God"?

What's it like to be God? What's it like to be the immovable mover? What's it like to be, always and always to have been? Was there ever a time when you experienced loneliness?

I've grown to know that I'm really happy when I'm around people who appreciate me and love me. You should be the happiest of all beings. But did you merely create all life forms as an expression of your love for life or did you do it so that you may be loved and appreciated? Please remember I'm writing this within a mere human perspective. Just the fact that you always were, are and always will be, boggles my mind. I've never experienced anything so phenomenal as that. How do you truthfully expect people to believe it? I'll try.

Wish I could write more.
With love beyond all other love,

Me

Dear ___,

You are merely human and can't comprehend all which is, isn't, has been and will be. I can. Trust me. I am total love. I am happiness. I am all. Just as you, I want to share myself with others. And just as you, I don't like frauds, lies, sinners and those who will hurt and take advantage of me selfishly. This is why I have created you. This is also why I test you—to see if you will or won't take advantage of me selfishly. You can't comprehend all that I am because you haven't even been associated with anyone that is like me.

You have been associated with what I have created, though. Believe in me and that which you haven't seen, because of everything you have seen. I am never bored, for I am companionship. You are not alone in what I ask of you. There have been others. Numbers beyond counting. People, larger in number than the grains of sand multiplied by infinity. I love and am love. And I wish to share this.

Trust me—

God

Dear Skeptic

Dear God,

    Why is there war, hatred, poverty, malnutrition, disease, adultery? How are we supposed to believe that you are all good when all that we see and read about is bad? How are we supposed to develop faith in you and your Church when every day priests and nuns are leaving their orders? Please, God, if you do exist and are all good, show us the way to goodness. Show us the way to your light. Show us the way to peace and love.

                Skeptic

Dear Skeptic,

    If I were to take away all of the bad things on earth, man would have no reason to strive for heaven. Heaven is the only place where life can be perfect. If I made it easy to get to heaven, even the undeserving people could make it. There must be sacrifice and pain before there can be the ultimate reward.

                God

Don't be so worried

Dear God,

 I am concerned about my future. When will I die? Would it be worth it to go to college and die after I graduate? Will I get married? Will I have a good wife, one whom I may love for all eternity? My kids—will I be able to be a good example to them? Will I be physically capable of having children? Have I seriously loved a girl? I'm partly sure, but there is no way to measure love and it's even harder to tell if you are truly in love. If I do get married and truly love a girl, will she die early and leave me heartbroken, or will I die and leave her heartbroken? Will I be able to support them? Will I be dead in five minutes or will I die in a car wreck in a year?

Dear Son,

 I cannot tell you when you're going to die. One should not be so obsessed with fear for the future. You should work for the life after death. Live each day as if you were going to live for 100 years. I shall guide you to the life after death. And be not tempted by the devil, the rejected one who tries to bring you to his own fate. Don't be so worried about life on earth.

     God

My doors are always open

Dear God,

    In spite of all the times I wondered why you took my little sister, I don't hate you for it. I didn't know her; I was too little. But perhaps, even though I didn't get a chance to grow up with her, I know her better than if I had. She's always there to turn to, to talk to, to confide in, and she'll always be there. That makes her special to me. She helps me out when I'm in trouble.

    Thank you for brightening my life with someone. I think he's something special. I know I don't appreciate him enough, but I've grown toward him. He brightens my day. I'm sorry for the times I've made him mad.

    Thank you also for my parents. They're really pretty understanding. They've done a good job in raising me so far. They've really put up with a lot of hell. Me being number six means they've been through a lot. They try to do what's best, even though I don't always agree with them. I'm sorry for all the times I felt like cursing them out, and just wish I was more grateful. I wish I appreciated the things they do for me more.

    Thank you also for my family. They're something else. They really care. We're really close and they mean a lot to me. I don't know what I'd do without them to stand behind me.

Dear ___,

    You know, it's really good to hear from you. I hope you know that your words and thoughts are always welcome. My doors are always open and my ears are always willing to listen.

    I'm glad you understand about your sister. I took her not out of hate, but out of love, and I think you realize that now. You see, you didn't lose a sister, you just have an extra-special one.

    I'm glad my person means something to you. He and everyone are something special and I'm glad you think so, too. I think now you've found an awfully good friend who will be there to talk to. It's awfully hard to find that someone on your way who is just for you.

    I'm glad that you feel that way about your family, especially your parents.

    God

You must live your life to the fullest

Dear Lord,

    I ask that you give my sister afflicted with cerebral palsy meaning in her life. To me, she seems lonely and helpless— meaning that her condition will never get any better; if anything, it will get worse. As you know, I prayed very hard as a young child that this thing would go away. But it never did. Through my adolescent years, I hated you for not curing my sister. I began to think you did this as a curse to our family. Now, though, I realize that by just going places in her wheelchair she brings people closer to you. I guess that her hell is on earth and her reward will be in heaven. Please let her know that you love her and let her know what she is here for.

Dear ____,

I made your sister the way she is so that she may be an example to others, so that others may realize their good health and all the other things about life. In this way they may live life to the fullest when they see your sister who can't. Your sister probably can't know her reason for being on earth. Don't let this bother you. You must live your own life to the fullest.

God

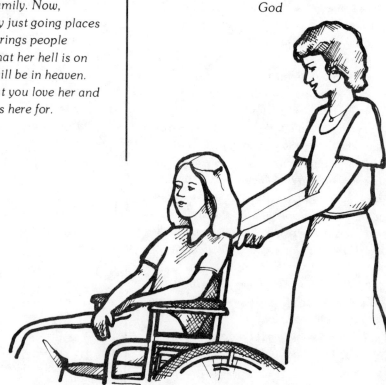

Let people love you

Lord,

    I don't know what to say. I just really want to tell someone, and especially you Lord, that I really am thankful for all the good things I have, and how much I love my family and friends. I'm beginning to appreciate all the good things in people, how different everyone is and how unique you are. I'm trying to love everyone.

    That's what I guess I want to say: I'm trying to do all the right things. I'm trying to overcome my fears and I'm really trying to be less jealous and selfish. The more I try to be the person I should be, the more I botch it all up. I usually just hurt the people I love the most. I expect them to go out of their way to help me and listen to my petty problems, instead of helping them.

    Remember when I asked for that second chance? I promised I'd change. I didn't, and I think you know that. You gave me the second chance, but I blew it. I got hurt and I hurt other people. Maybe with lots of your help I could have a third chance, and we can make it work. If someone would just say that they understood and that they saw I was trying; that I was important to them; that I'm their friend — then I could really start to be their friend.

I know I've asked a lot — but isn't that what you're all about and what friends are for?

                    Yours truly . . .

Dear _____,

Well, kid, I heard you; I was listening and I understand. I know that you are trying and I know that you know that you're something special, and so is everyone else. You know, maybe someday you'll get that third chance, if it's the best thing for you. People care for you a great deal, if only you'd get off their case for a while. I love you and you're blessed: You've got all the good things in life. Expect much, but don't be disappointed. Don't force people to love you; let them love.

    About that third chance: Take it easy, let my will and nature take their course. I know you are trying; let people love you. I do.

            Love,

            God

Suggestions for Discussion and Dialogue

Reflect on what it has been like to complete the various exercises in this book. Ask yourself if you have changed or grown in any way—either in your own self-awareness and prayer life or in your relationship with the person with whom you have been sharing these exercises. Become conscious, too, of what God has been saying to you in this process.

Exercise 11
Write brief answers to the following questions:

1)   Which pair of letters (to and *from* God) struck you the most? Why?

2)   If you were God, would you have answered any of the letters in this section differently? Write out what you would say.

3)   How do the people who wrote these letters seem to feel about God? What image comes across in the letters *from* God?

4)   Would you describe your prayer as a one-way conversation or as a dialogue? How would you go about making your prayer life more of a dialogue with God?

Exercise 12
As a final exercise, imagine what God would most want to say to you if he were sitting in the room with you now. Write a letter from God to yourself. Afterwards, reflect on how you feel about what your God had to say to you.

Suggested Reading

Moral Development: A Guide to Piaget and Kohlberg, by Ronald Duska and Mariellen Whelan. New York: Paulist Press, 1975.

"Toward a Developmental Perspective on Faith," by James Fowler. *Religious Education* (LXIX): March-April, 1974, 207-219.

"Faith, Liberation, and Human Development," by James Fowler. *Foundations* (LXXIX): Spring, 1974, 1-33.

"Stage and Sequence: The Cognitive Developmental Approach to Socialization," by Lawrence Kohlberg. *Handbook of Socialization Theory and Research*, edited by R.A. Hoslin. Chicago: Rand-McNally, 1969, 347-400.

Religious Education and the Life-Cycle, by Lawrence Losoncy. Bethlehem, Pa.: Catechetical Communications, 1977.

The Moral Development of the Child, by Jean Piaget. New York: The Free Press, 1965.

Readings in Moral Education, edited by Peter Scharf. Minneapolis: Winston Press, 1978.